BECOMING UNB

Tables des matières

Becoming Unbreakable

3 Simple Principles To Knowing Exactly Who You Are, Taking Control Of How You Feel And Making What Seems Impossible A Reality

Simon Gwilliam

"I'm no longer ruled by time and overwhelm. I've given up on negative thinking and feeling guilty about everyday stuff. My confidence in myself has grown and I am trying new stuff and being pushed, which I love."

"Started my new business. Published my book. Improved my mindset, energy, and how I feel inside. Before I was always in survival and I didn't even know - I can feel the difference now. I feel different inside - calmer, more neutral, almost empty, but not in a bad way because I can draw up whatever feelings I want to feel, whenever I want to feel them. I can recognise when I'm getting stressed and frazzled and pushing too hard, and then take steps to slow down and re-focus".

"My mental strength raised massively. I'm no longer the victim of my thoughts. The feeling of freedom is priceless. When I watch these rushing people, I realise how free I feel. No more guilt for who I am. Acceptance and appreciation for life and beautiful nature."

"I am now learning to trust myself and others bit more now. Loving myself again and finding who I am again. I have truly 'let - go' of a traumatic event which occurred 4 years ago (to the point I give it no thought. It's as if it happened to somebody else.) I deeply believe that no matter what major / minor setbacks I encounter in life, I will be absolutely fine because I will deal effectively with whatever is occurring."

"I no longer over - value the opinions of others and therefore have no inclination to people - please. I have become my BETTER self not my FAKE self and this is immensely freeing. Frankly, I am beginning to flourish in every aspect of my life. Unbreakable has emboldened my courageous streak, heightened my energy levels and improved the quality of my thoughts."

"I have started living again- no longer stuck & held hostage in my grief. I have overcome my physical condition of trigeminal neuralgia known as the suicide disease that held my whole life hostage. I have travelled and had adventures and made progress with the course I'm doing."

"Moving on from the past and past relationship-s being able to let it go. Becoming more confident in my job role and being able to manage how people affect me better. Learning to not let things bother me and that when things happen that are bad, I'm able to see it then deal with how I can move forward from it without becoming overwhelmed and taking to my bed with migraines and exhaustion from overthinking."

"I got out of the house and went on little walks. I am back driving. I went on a little camping holiday with my husband and kids- something I couldn't imagine doing before I started Unbreakable because I was a person who couldn't leave my house and now every chance I get I'm getting out of the house and going on days out and having fun and making happy memories with my family. I can't thank you enough for how much you have helped me so far. I'm a much happier person and my kids and everyone around me have noticed the change in me. Thanks again."

Table of Contents:

To get the best out of life you have to get the best out of yourself'.

To all the Unbreakables out there, thank you for being part of something that is transforming so many lives. Without you, this system would never exist, and we would have no voice.

Thank you.

To one in particular. Thank you for showing me what is important, believing in me even when I may have doubted myself and for standing by my side.

And of course Murph Man.. the Original Unbreakable

INTRODUCTION.

Whatever is going on for you right now, I am going to presume you have picked this book up with the intention of changing something.

Maybe you are doing pretty damn well, and you want to take your success to 'the next level'.

Maybe you are really struggling and are desperate to make some serious changes.

Or maybe, just maybe, you have been given it by someone who obviously thinks a lot of you.

Whether or not you want to improve your body, your mind, how you feel, a relationship or even your business or career; the system on the following pages will help you.

It's tried.

It's tested.

A thousand people have gone through this system and made changes that they never thought possible.

Olympians, multi-million-pound business owners, people going through loss, struggling with how they feel about themselves, folks who wanted to overcome their anxieties and move past that feeling of being stuck, all using it to move to the next best stage in their life.

Everyone who enters our program now fills in a start form asking them where they rate themselves in key areas such as;

Energy Levels

Body Image

Anxiety Levels

Stress levels

Happiness

Quality of Thoughts and more...

We then ask the same questions at the end of 30 days or routinely throughout.

91% of people report a drastic increase in energy levels

91.7 % of people see drastic reductions in anxiety

98.4% of people report a drastic reduction in stress levels

92.3 of people saw a dramatic increase in their happiness

94.4 % of people say a dramatic increase in the quality of their thoughts

Of course, this begs the question; what happened to the other people? Many arrived not wanting an increase in those things and already feeling content enough in those particular areas. We help people who are in a good place which they want to make even better, just as much as those who are struggling.

Why do I share this with you? Because this is real data, from real people, reporting real change.

Our methods work.

I personally used it to achieve things I could only have dreamed of.

Now it's your turn.

However, there is something I really want to get across to you in the intro here. In a world where we are becoming more and more obsessed with looking to something outside of us to solve our problems or give us the answers, this book is going to encourage you to look to yourself.

When you get the best out of yourself you will get the best out of what it is you are trying to improve.

When you get the best out of yourself you will experience one of the greatest feelings in your life, a feeling much stronger than happiness – fulfilment.

You will transform in front of your very eyes.

We will be going on a journey together... a journey of upgrade. Not because you are broken, oh no, but because you have the desire to get better and you need no other reason than that.

We will cover:

The Three Truths. Unless we can accept these truths, change cannot happen.

The Unbreakable Journey. The journey Unbreakables go on when they want to make changes to anything in life.

The Three Struggles. Struggles that always stop us from completing that journey and the Unbreakable System to overcome them along with other struggles and setbacks that you may encounter.

It's time for you to BE who you want.

It's time to become Unbreakable.

CHAPTER 1

The Three Truths

There are three truths to getting the best out of yourself.

Any significant or meaningful results in your life will be hindered by an unwillingness to accept these three truths.

1 – You are a creator.

2 – You always have a choice

3 – You are 100% responsible for your life

Now before you start trying to question them...

Let's take a look at them first.

TRUTH 1

You are a creator

This is the truth that I want you to embrace fully. It is a truth that so many have forgotten.

There are two models of living that I can say I have tried.

1 – Is to live as a reactive participant

This is the, 'everything is happening to me' mode that I spent most of the first part of my life in. It generally involves a ton of waiting about for things to change before we feel how we want.

I spent years waiting for things to line up perfectly before I took any action. (Needless to say, very little action occurred!) I spent even longer blaming what was going on around me for how I felt inside.

In the most brutal sense this can be best described as being a victim to life.

It got me nowhere. Well that is a lie. It got me to where I was and kept me there, participating in a life that I felt I had no say or control over.

My Wonderful Dad, (You will hear a lot about him in this book) has a lot of wisdom in his directness. I remember him saying;

'It can't always be about everyone else you know'

He wasn't far wrong. After all, even if we can look for justification in how rough we have had it, does that move us forward?

For me and the tons of people we now train in our Unbreakable system, it's very easy to sit and wait and even blame the things we have no control over for our lack in life.

However, it is much more enjoyable and productive to focus on what you can control, and that is where model two comes along.

2 – To live as an ACTIVE creator.

Look around you. Look at nature. Look at life. Birth, death, ageing and the way we live; life by definition is ever evolving and moving.

Yet, as human beings, we seem resigned to staying the same even though there is part of us that really does desire something different.

You can feel it right? The pull towards wanting something more, something different.

This is not a theological tract by any stretch, but it is worth noting that the three main mono-theistic religions, (Christianity, Judaism and Islam) all describe, in one way or another, God creating man in His image.

Genesis Ch1 vs27; "God created man in the image of Himself, in the image of God He crated him, male and female He created them."

Some would read this as meaning, among other things, that God created us as creators ourselves.

Whether you follow a faith, are an atheist, or anything in between, this would suggest that for at least a couple of thousand years, people have recognised the fact that we, as humans, are creators.

Being human intrinsically means being creative. Humans are the only species that can imagine and then bring into existence what they imagine.

It would be reasonable to say that by not recognising our creative selves, we our doing our humanity a disservice.

Zen Bhuddist roshi John Loori: "Being creative is our birth right. It is an integral part of being human, as basic as walking, talking and thinking."

Due to the creative spark that all humans have, that YOU have, we frequently desire more than our current circumstance. We can feel a sense of frustration with our reality…. this does not have to be a non-negotiable state. You are here to create what you want!

This quote from Ayn Rand sums it up perfectly; "Do not let your fire go out, spark by irreplaceable spark in the hopeless swamps of the not quite, the not yet and the not at all. Do not let the hero in your soul perish in lonely frustration for the life you deserved and have never been able to reach. The world you desire can be won. It exists... it is real.... It is possible... it's yours." (Atlas Shrugged, 1957)

You are here to grow.

You are here to experience life.

You are here to create it.

You are a creator.

You have the power to create the life you want.

The first step towards that is to accept the role of active creator in your own life. After all, why would we want it any other way? Perhaps so that we have something to blame for where we are?

When I personally took on the responsibility of being the creator in my life, things started to change fast for me, I also felt the most in control of my destiny than ever before.

Believe me, you are always creating. With every word you speak, thought you have, and action you take you are creating your life. Humans are so powerful we can imagine something different for ourselves and go make that happen.

We just forget. In a world where so much seems out of our control, we forget how much control we have over ourselves. We doubt our ability to make things happen and in so doing, start to look outside of us to things we have no control over at all, and that is where the trouble starts. This is where we become a victim to life.

We now feel the helpless sensation of being a participant in a game that we can't seem to win.

If 'Becoming Unbreakable' stands for anything. It stands for creation.

It's here to remind you that you are powerful. That if you look around you right now there are so many things in your life that once didn't exist, and you made them happen.

That is all the proof you need to know that you can create.

Unbreakable is about creation, and I am proud to say hundreds of people a month use our system to create. This book isn't about my story. There are enough books pedaling motivational stories. It's about giving you the practical tools to create something better for yourself.

But first of all, you must accept-

YOU are a creator.

This first truth is the most fundamental and is dependent upon you recognising and accepting two further truths: That you always have a choice and that you are 100% responsible

TRUTH 2

You always have a choice

About 2 months ago, I wrote a Facebook post. It said the following:

"Staying stuck is a choice, one you can change in an instant"

It was popular - except someone took offence to it:

"If only we were all that selfish. Then you are right, we could be happy"

Now, I am not one of those people who attacks anyone with a different opinion to mine, so I sat and looked at it and wrote the following:

"Thanks for joining in. What about not choosing to stay stuck is selfish?"

The reply?

"That's what the man down the road thought before he left his partner and three kids on their own."

I thought about it and wrote back explaining how a similar thing had happened to someone I knew very well. How, in the long run, things worked out a lot better than if the couple in question had stayed in an unhappy relationship that was miserable for both of them.

Shortly after this, I realised something. The quote wasn't written for the man that chose to leave. It was written for the woman who now chose to stay stuck and powerless.

You cannot control the cards life gives you, and as we know, life will deal you a cruel hand at times. You won't like the choices that are available to you but refusing to see that you have a choice at all will keep you stuck.

Your situation may seem hopeless. But I would ask you, is your situation hopeless, or have you become hopeless about your situation? There is a big difference. You always, ALWAYS have choices that you can make, and choosing the next best option will always get you better results than refusing to believe you have one at all.

Your future can be changed by one decision. One choice can offset a lifetime of seemingly insurmountable crap. BUT YOU HAVE TO CHOOSE.

If you want to change your results, remember you are always choosing. You will start taking back power in your life. Be it in your body, mind, family or business. You always have a choice.

TRUTH 3

You are 100% responsible

In March 2017 a lady started to email me regularly. She wanted me to help her move forward in her life. I'll be honest, at the time I was reluctant. She emailed about once a week and would tell me about her life, her past and how she saw no way forward.

Her story was a tough one; her past filled with wrongdoing, hurt and anger that she was still carrying around with her every day.

So, we made a pact.

It was this: regardless of what had happened she would take 100% responsibility for where she was now. This is not to say that the things that had happened to her were her fault. Don't confuse responsibility in this case with blame. Responsibility, in this instance, is being accountable for both your choice as to how you are going to move forward and for the creation of your future reality. I have no doubt it was one of the hardest things for her to do, and it was certainly a struggle. Things in life may not be your fault. You may have had no say in them whatsoever, but the responsibility to do what's best for you afterwards is all yours.

Taking responsibility is one of the most freeing experiences of your life. No blame, no fault, no shame. Just you; taking responsibility for what you do from that point forward.

Response--Ability is how I choose to look at it.

12 months later, the lady that got in touch with me is nowhere to be seen.

When we speak now, she is smiling and happy. Relationships that were gone are restored and relationships she never thought possible are blossoming.

She has taken back control of her life, and it happened the moment she took responsibility for it.

You can't control what happens in most of life.

You can always control how you deal with things and move on.

Take 100% Response – Ability.

CHAPTER 2

The Journey of Change

Funny word that, 'change' isn't it? It's becoming a bit taboo these days. People really don't like to think we have to change. The problem is, that's what getting new results requires! After all, if you don't change something, then you can't expect to get something different, can you?

Anyways, I digress. Change is what you are here for and change always involves this journey:

Moving from

Point A (where you are starting)

To

Point B (where you want to end up)

Yet it can be so hard don't you think? Change isn't easy, and there is a real reason why.

Change requires you to be greater than your current reality. It may be worth reading that again, because it's that important. OK I'll say it again.

Change requires you to BE greater than your current reality.

After all you can't do the same things and expect a different result can you. Einstein said it best.

"The definition of insanity is to keep doing the same thing and expect a different result."

So, how can we BE greater than our current REALITY? Well it might help to start by defining REALITY.

If we can say that our current reality is our circumstance, environment and everything in our life right now as it is.

Then we have to BE greater than that to make the changes we want.

So, what do we mean by BE?

A state of BEING is defined as how we are thinking, feeling, and acting.

So, we have to think, feel, and act greater than we do right now to create a change in our life.

That is why change is hard. How can I be greater than my current reality before it has changed?

How can I think and feel greater than my reality when I am feeling overwhelmed and stressed about my workload?

How can I go and exercise or have that tough conversation or just get out and about when I'm exhausted or scared of failing?

How can I get out in to the unknown when I can't find the courage to take the first step?
In Unbreakable we have 3 distinct steps and phases to go through

STEP 1 – THE VEIL

STEP 2 – THE VOID

STEP 3 – THE VICTORY

When you see how these phases can hinder you when trying to make change, and then learn the 3 keys to overcoming these stumbling blocks and becoming greater than your reality, you will find that you start making your changes a reality pretty pronto.

STEP 1

The Veil

The veil is the point at which you go to step in to the unknown. Maybe it is applying for a job, asking someone out, joining the gym, or even just taking the step to do something new. All of a sudden you start talking yourself out of it.

That my friend is the VEIL. You know how it goes. The little voice creeps in,

'I haven't got time.'
'What if I fail, or look stupid?'
'I'm too tired.'
'I'm not that bothered anyway – things aren't so bad.'

Before we know it, we are back to doing what we always do and getting what we always have.

We all have a veil that comes down when we go about stepping out of our zone of normal. You may have heard of the saying;

'When things are good you see people's personality, when tough, you find their character'

I like that saying, but I've also found that the further we get away from what is 'normal' for us, the more the Veil comes in to play. It wants to keep you safe, even if safe isn't really what you want. It's crazy how we would rather stay in a position we don't like rather than go out and risk going after what we do.

There is a popular experiment conducted with fleas which is used by many authors and speakers which I think illustrates the limiting power of the Veil perfectly.

In an experiment, a scientist placed a number of fleas in a glass jar. They quickly jumped out. The scientist then placed a glass lid over the jar. The fleas continued to jump, only now they were hitting the glass lid and were and falling back down into the jar. After some time, the fleas started jumping to a height just below the lid in order to avoid hitting it. The scientist then removed the lid of the jar entirely. Instead of jumping to freedom, the fleas, now conditioned to limit themselves from jumping beyond the height of the lid, did not escape but continued to jump fruitlessly to a height just below their chance of freedom.

The Veil does that to you. It keeps where you are. It keeps you believing you can't jump out in to the unknown. As in the case of the glass lid, it is a deception. The Veil is built on fears and old patterns that don't help you, and instead keep you stuck where you are.

Your key to change. Is noticing the Veil for what it is: your imagination and old programs. From there you can step beyond it and step in to into what we call the Void

STEP 2

The Void

The Void is the space between where you are and where you want to be, and if you want to change your results it's a space we must step in to.

It's the space that the Veil tries to keep you from entering, and there is good reason. Because the Void is the land of possibility. It's where you are free to BE whoever you choose. It's by stepping beyond the Veil that we can start to take new actions and create a new future.

That is why change is so hard my friend, because we have to first deal with our conditioning; The Veil of old doubts, old programs and beliefs about ourselves and then step into this unknown Void.

The Void could be described as a no man's land. It's a bit of a risk, and we humans generally try to avoid risk. We find it easier to stay in the safety of what we have. "Better the Devil you know….." Even if what we have and where we are sucks, because at least we know what we are getting. We cling to our known circumstances instead of embracing the unknown of an exciting future.

I was someone who never entered that Void. I had great ideas, I had dreams and I had times where things weren't working for me and yet I still wouldn't step into the Void and that, right there, is how we really stop ourselves from living and achieving the results we really want.

Because remember what we said:

'Change requires us to be greater than our current reality. '

Being greater than our current reality involves stepping out of our current reality and into that unknown space.

The Unbreakable Focus section goes into much more depth as to why the Void is so important. Until then know this:

The Void is something you can learn to love and no longer be afraid of. It's not something to be rushed through and battled against. It's something to be embraced.

The void is your friend. The more you embrace it the better it gets.

STEP 3

Victory

Victory is landing at point B. It's seeing the changes you wanted so badly come to fruition. Most people never appreciate their arrival at point B, because they don't see the changes they have made.

You may have done this in your own life: worked hard, made lots of changes, but you still feel like it is not enough. Or you just can't see the changes that you have already made.

I have spoken at length about creation. To create what you want, you will naturally have a goal in mind. A place that you want to be, a target that you want to reach. We do it in many aspects of our life... it's natural, it's a creative way to live, it's human. We crave progress or change in so many areas;

Our bodies – "If I could just drop a few more lbs THEN I'll be happy."

Money – "I just want a little more and then life will be so much easier."

Partners – "If they would just do 'x', then our relationship would be so much better."

To want different is great, it's fine and it's basically why we are here. BUT…. In your pursuit of progress do not make the mistake of only looking forward and never looking back at how far you have come. In Unbreakable, we encourage you to aim forwards and measure backwards. Do not do yourself the disservice of failing to notice your personal progress, however big or small that may be.

It may be the smallest of changes, the littlest of steps... but it is imperative that you take stock and see all the areas in which you have been Victorious! You have reached that point B many times over, don't miss out on VICTORY because you fail to notice it.

So, there you have the Unbreakable Journey.

Moving from Point A through the Veil, into the Void and finally being Victorious.

Now you have some sort of an idea, or map, of the Unbreakable journey. You know that change requires you to be greater than your current reality and to be greater than your current reality you have to move beyond the Veil, embrace the Void and notice your Victories. In the following chapters, I will outline the struggles that one generally encounters while navigating the Void and the tools that Unbreakables use to overcome them. A system to 'Becoming Unbreakable'

Chapter 3

The Three Struggles Of Change

Struggle 1

Not being able to see beyond where you are

It's now the modern trend to talk about and share struggles, which is great, and I mean that. It really is a great start to open up about where we are and hear others do the same.

It allows us to not feel so isolated and awareness will always help create change. Now, with social media it's easier than ever to share these things.

Again – It's a great thing, I'm not knocking it, but it comes with a problem.......

When the conversation stays around that and doesn't move forward, neither do we. You become stuck; not able to see beyond the point that you are at. The more you talk about and focus on how tough your current situation is, the more embedded in it you become.

It doesn't matter what your struggle is; be it in a bad place and trying to move away from that, or in a decent place wanting better and struggling to move towards that.

Maybe it's your body, your mind, your finances or business. It's all the same thing. The more we talk about where we are, the more we read about where we are, the more we fill our brains with the problems related to our current situation and the stronger we make those FEELINGS of struggle. Which leads to a problem.

People a lot smarter than me have figured something out

'You can't think greater than how you FEEL'

Feel sad... think sad thoughts.

Feel stressed... think stressed thoughts.

Feel anxious... think anxious thoughts.

Feel afraid... think fear-based thoughts.

So, the more we think about our problems, the more we focus on where we are and how hard it is for us, the more we feel those feelings of struggle.

Your actions are always a reflection of how you feel, so yep, you guessed it; you stay stuck taking the same actions and getting the same results.

We are literally clinging to where we are, not able to see beyond our own obsession with our personal struggles. We are reinforcing our life as it is, with our own struggle narrative; the negative commentary on our life that is a constant companion to us the more we fuel it with our attention. From that point it can feel impossible to move forward in any positive way.

This shows up a lot when people first start in our programs and I ask the question, 'What would you like to get from the next 30 days?' The answers, 'I don't want to....'' and, "No more........" and, "I need to stop......" always pop up. Notice here that these are all statements based in the negative. I rarely hear, "I'd like to...." and "I want more...." Or "I want to feel...." What I mean by this is that the more you focus on what you DON'T want, the more power t has over you. By focusing on what you believe is wrong/missing/unsatisfactory about yourself, the more embedded in your vision of yourself this negativity becomes. It is really hard to then see beyond that vision and towards any improved future.

Muhammad Ali said, 'The hands can't hit what the eyes can't see.' Granted, he was talking about boxing, however, he's right; you can't hit what you can't see. You can't be greater than your current reality if you don't know what greater than your current reality is.

So, what is the answer to moving past this problem? How can you let go of where you are and take the first step to moving towards a brighter future full of the results you want?

You have to create a vision of the future you do want.

A vision about you and your life. About how it looks, and more importantly how it feels. A vision reinforced with positive emotions that inspire you to change because then you have something to work towards. This vision is not about what you DON'T want; it is all about what you DO want.

Without a positive vision of the future, all that is left is what you have now. That just keeps us stuck, feeling the same way, making the same choices, taking the same actions and getting the same results. We don't want that. We want new. We want different. That starts with a new vision.

So, before we go on, let's recap.

To create change we have to BE greater than our current reality. To get a new result in life we have to experience the Void.

The first struggle we have in going from where we are to where we want to be and creating new results is our habit of not seeing beyond our current situation. To be greater than our current reality we have to know what greater looks like.

The biggest problem we have with this is our constant reinforcement of where we are, and not where we want to be.

Creating a positive VISION of your future is how we go about this.

A vision is not a goal. A vision is much more than that.

Solution 1

Unbreakable Vision

When I was in primary school, I watched a great film. Cool Runnings. I loved it so much I watched it every day of the holidays. It's about a top Jamaican sprinter who trips in his trials and isn't allowed to go to the Olympics.

Cut a long story short and he's persuading an ex Olympic Gold medalist in bobsleigh to teach him and his mates so they can go to the Winter Olympics.

John Candy plays the coach and is an American legend who had his gold medals taken away for cheating. Fast forward most of the film and, much to the world's surprise, they are not only in the Olympics but are in with a chance of winning a Medal. The night before the final run the main character asks the coach a question.

"Coach, why did you cheat? You had an Olympic Gold medal, you had it all."

The answer: "Darice. A Gold Medal is a wonderful thing but if you aren't enough without it, you will never be enough with it."

What was the great John Candy saying? He was saying;

<u>Who you are, is always more important than what you have.</u>

That is the difference between a goal and a vision. A goal says I want to lose X lbs. or earn X amount of money or not feel like this. It's all about the END. It's all about WHAT we will have. A goal is one dimensional.

A vision starts with WHO, not what. A Vision is 3 dimensional. Why do we start with who? Well think about it, the reason we do anything is because of the way we think it will make us feel. That is the sole reason we desire anything different, because we think we will feel better for having it.

Yet how often do we hit our goals and feel no different? All the time, right? That's how the person who sets out to lose a few stone in the hope of liking who they see in the mirror, can lose all that weight and still not like who they see. It's why the perfect partner can still leave you feeling unloved, and the perfect house and money situation can still leave you feeling empty.

Because as John Candy says...

'If you aren't enough without it, you will never be enough with it.'

Rather than waiting to see if something external can fulfil us, why don't we take control and go and create what we desire?

Additionally, rather than waiting to be told who we are; allowing others to define us, why don't we take back control and define ourselves? That's the first part of creating a vision: Deciding who you want to be.

We don't try and 'find' ourselves in Unbreakable. WE CREATE OURSELVES.

Because you will never outperform your identity. You will never achieve greater than how you define yourself.

So, who do you want to be? That is the question.

Not long ago, I went to my neighbour's funeral. He was 84 years old and an incredible man. Rather than do anyone a disservice and try and put that into words, I'm going to say this; At any funeral I have been to, all people talk about is WHO that person was. They recount memories, moments. They talk about people's character, and that is what we remember: WHO people were.

We don't talk about what they had, we rarely mention material things, and yet so much of people's lives is spent focusing on that, to the detriment of our health, well-being and our values.

I'm not saying having material things is bad. I love nice things. Nice things won't, however, make up for who you AREN'T. Which is why excess is out of control in the modern world, as we look more and more to external things to make us feel better.

The whole theme of my programs became this a long time ago. 'Be WHO you want to BE' because when we do that everything else seems to follow along nicely.
'But I don't know who I am!' is something that I hear all the time.

My question:

WHO do you WANT to BE?

Because that seems to be what life is all about.

It's a question that needs answering honestly. Not based on who we think we ought to be, who we think others think we should be, what's deemed acceptable by society or what we think is possible. Who do YOU want to be?

After you have decided who you want to be, it's now time to decide why. Now I know your 'why' is talked about a lot these days. The old, 'You gotta know your why' kinda stuff is bandied around loads. We, however, are going a different route with it. Your why is how you want to feel when you get there. So how do you want to feel when you arrive at being this person? Will you feel confident, healthy, powerful, enough, strong, determined, loved, loving. How do you want to feel?

Let's think what happens when most people set out to change something.

Say we decide to get fit. We say, 'I want to be able to fit in to my new jeans'. That's as far as we go usually. That's the goal, but then we do something we don't realise. We start attaching negative emotions to the pursuit of that goal.

48

We attach the feeling of dread at having to start training or managing our diet. We tell ourselves it's going to be hard work. We attach a lot of sacrifice to it and all of a sudden, our initial motivation drops, and we end up hating the process all together.

It's the same process whatever goal we set. Be it mental health, financial or anything in between.

Instead we are going to attach some positive emotions to our target, so we have something to shift our focus to.

How will you feel when you get there? Will you feel accomplished, confident, successful, free, happy?

Step one is WHO?
Step two is WHY?

Step 3 is the last, and it's WHAT? What do I want all this to look like?

By this I mean what sort of things will you be doing?

When people come to me and tell me that they are really struggling, that they are so anxious that they can't leave the house, I will always lead them to describe how they want to be feeling. I encourage them further; to think about what they would be doing if they felt the way they had described to me. What would they be doing if they left the house every day? What would they LIKE to be doing?

When I set a goal to increase my fitness or take on a challenge, I outline how that will look day to day to me.

The key word is LIKE. What would you like to be doing day to day? How would you be acting? If you were being this person and feeling the way you set out, what would you be doing?

So, if you answer those three questions you will have a vision. You will know who you want to be, you will know how you want that to feel, and you will know how you will be acting that day.

That's the kind of vision that gets you to stop clinging to where you are and enables you to see a future beyond your current situation. That's the kind of vision that moves you across the Void.

It is fueled by who you want to be and how you want to feel, not by who you don't want to be.
It is fueled by desire, not dissatisfaction.

It's a vision that you could imagine and almost taste. It's a vision you can now start to make a reality.

Action Step 1

Create Your Vision

The best exercise I have ever used for creating my vision is 'The Perfect Day.'

You simply write out what your perfect day would look like using as much detail as possible. Using all your senses. What would you see? What would you smell? What would you hear? Where would you wake up? Who with? How would you go about your day? And how would that feel? You need so much depth that if I was to find it and read it, I could experience it myself.

Take your time. Sit down and write your perfect day out. Don't limit it by what you think is possible. Fire up your imagination and don't forget the feelings. It's all about the feelings.

Struggle 2

Running on Empty and

Living in Survival

In January of this year I started working with Andrea, a former Olympian who was struggling, in her own words with 'burnout'. Now working in a high position in the corporate world, she was at a point where she could barely get out of bed, she was working less than 50% and struggling. Emotionally exhausted and mentally drained, she couldn't see a way out.

I call this Running on Empty. Where we have nothing left to give to anyone let alone ourselves. It's impossible to make it across the Void to our new results when we have nothing in the tank.

Exhaustion is the new epidemic.

Our jobs, our commitments and our lifestyle are so full-on that all our power goes to other people and we are left with the dregs. A huge amount of the feelings we experience day to day such as anxiety and overwhelm can be attributed to exhaustion. We are literally walking around with our fuel gauge on empty, wondering why we feel so crap. The worst part is, at this point you blame yourself. You say, 'I just don't have any willpower. I need to get more motivation; I don't want it enough.' The reality? We are exhausted, and when we are exhausted nothing seems to be appealing. We can't seem to get going for anything.

Imagine for a minute that you have a glass of water. In fact, go and get one and fill it halfway up. Go on.... This will help you make sense of this I promise.

Ok, now you have got it. Imagine the water represents your energy levels and pour a little bit away. You have less, right? That water pouring away represents you giving your energy to your day to day life; work and family etc. Now imagine you need to give some to your friend as she has a few problems she wants help with. Pour away a little more. Less, again right?

OK imagine something big is going on in your life, something has come up and it's a massive worry and pour all of what is left away. Now you have nothing left. You are officially on empty!

Every day we are giving our energy to things, to people, to family, work and life. Yet we reach the point where we have nothing left and still expect to be able to make changes in our life. It's impossible. Of course, at this point you will beat yourself up for not having enough motivation or willpower, but the reality is you are just exhausted. You are running on empty.

It's important to note that I'm not talking just physically exhausted. Sure, we know most people are tired from poor sleep, diet and lack of daily movement. That's just part of it.

You actually have three types of energy that are running on empty and causing us problems:

Physical, Mental and Emotional. Think of how much mental energy we are using each and every day. Did you know we have between 60-70 thousand thoughts a day? Of which 90% are the same day after day? I'm sure you are also aware that your thoughts have a massive impact on your life.

We wake up and immediately find ourselves thinking the same usual thoughts. We start thinking of everything we have to get done that day, maybe check our phone and go through Facebook or our work emails and waste a ton of energy there. We race about dropping people off or driving to work; thinking about the meeting we have or worrying about that argument we had last night.

It's no wonder we are exhausted, our thoughts are causing us so much stress and are draining our energy.

What about emotionally? Well, all these thoughts we have about the future cause us to create feelings, right? We often start thinking about the future and what could go wrong, and we feel stressed, our heart races, we might even get anxious or afraid. We are emotionally draining ourselves with our own mind. These panic-driven and reactionary feelings about future events have nothing to do with the Vision of the future that we want! It is said that 70% of the average human's life is spent in a state we call 'Survival.'

Survival states are things such as, overwhelm, anxiety, doubt, fear and stress.

The modern human can experience these intense emotions while in some pretty passive states. Your heart can race when you are sat with a cuppa thinking about an upcoming meeting, you can seethe with anger or cry with heartbreak while lying on your sofa.

Evolution designed and fine-tuned our emotions, however, for action and for movement. A hangover from our hunter-gatherer past, which in the scheme of things wasn't that long ago, is that any intense EMOTIONAL feeling can propel us into Survival; a state in which we experience both emotional and physical 'side effects.'

To be healthy and functional, we need to be able to feel and connect to all of our emotions at different times, even the less pleasant ones. Survival-mode emotions and responses are necessary.

Think of an animal in the wild, out and about eating its grass and living the dream. All of a sudden, it spots a predator stalking it. It goes into survival-mode.

Firstly, it mobilizes lots of survival chemicals in its body to deal with the threat, its heart speeds up, adrenalin is released and all that jazz.

Then it takes a look around it's environment, it focuses on the threat and looks for a solution.

Lastly it starts thinking of time. How long have I got to get there? How close is the threat? We are no different to this. If you have just walked into a rough part of town, and see a group of lads swinging baseball bats on a street corner, you may well feel some fear, you may well mobilize those survival chemicals and you may well get the hell out of there! Good! In this instance, you need that fear to help your safety and survival.

It is thought that the average modern human is walking around in that state for 70% of their life. Except there is no predator. Our thoughts and anxieties are turning this process on. We start to worry about 'what if' and our body goes in to stress, our heart speeds up, and we feel the energy rushing about. Our awareness narrows and we focus on immediate problems in our own world. This only serves to feed the situation more. Finally, we become very aware of time. We start to predict a time in the future that this feeling will end, thus pushing feeling good away even further.

It's no wonder it's hard to change is it? 70% of the time we are looking to stay safe.

The problem with Survival is that it's not a time to create anything new, it's a time to protect what you have and stay safe. That is why it's killing your chances of changing anything, it's rooting you to the spot.

So here we are running on empty and living in Survival and trying to fight against that to create changes.

So, this is where we start.

There is nothing more important than how you feel.

Sure, you may argue that how your kids feel is more important and I do get the point. However, to try helping them be happy and confident when you are stressed, run down and emotionally all over the shop is a fool's game my friend. It isn't happening.

You really can't help anyone if you can't help yourself. The biggest gift you can give anyone you care about is the display of your own happiness, your own confidence and your own wellbeing. Trust me, they are watching and modelling everything they see.

That is where Andrea and I started. We set about filling that glass back up using the simple daily steps in Unbreakable we call the Power Points.

12 months later and I had the pleasure of meeting Andrea face to face in London after she travelled over from Oslo.

Smiling, happy, full of energy, full of life, out skiing again. She's doing voluntary work and creating her own ski coaching business as well as qualifying as a personal trainer. She is back in control of her life, happy in her relationships and living life on her terms. A huge difference from not being able to get out of bed for 6 months. It's all come about through raising her mental, physical and emotional power levels.

Running on empty and living in survival will keep you stuck.

It shows up as a lack of willpower and motivation.

It leads to overwhelm, anxiety, stress and exhaustion.

It STOPS you BEING greater than your current reality.

The answer is:

Creating as much Energy as possible.

Solution 2

Unbreakable Energy

In Unbreakable we have a daily system that we follow to create the most powerful version of you possible, getting you out of Survival and into Creation scoring points along the way much like a game. The trouble is, that is a thirty-day course in itself, so I'm going to break them in to some simple routines you can plug in to your life straight away.

So, what is Unbreakable Energy and how do you create it?

Unbreakable Energy is investing daily in the three energy systems.

Mind - Mental Energy
Body - Physical Energy
Soul - Emotional Energy

Most folks I come across either rarely take the time to invest in any or mainly use their body to feel better, so at best you are running at ⅓ power.

We will start with Body. After all its everyone's favourite right?! At this point you may be thinking that you haven't got time to go to the gym, or you are happy with how you look etc. That's not the reason we invest in our body. We want energy. We want physical energy flowing around us. We do this in two simple ways;

MOVEMENT

Like I said earlier, most people are tired, and at this point convince themselves that they need a rest. Resting is not what most people need; it's more movement. Think of your body as a car battery that charges when you use it, want more energy? Start creating it by moving.

WATER OR GREENS

The second thing we do with our body is hydrate it. Again, most people think of water as a tool for weight loss or something like that. For us it's to help our brain function better. Brain fog is a huge problem these days with our heads feeling fuzzy and all over the shop, feeling like we can't concentrate and having those mid-afternoon slumps. A huge factor is dehydration. So, in Unbreakable we set out to drink more water. You will be surprised how much more energy you will feel from just doing this. As a side note, if you ever feel anxious or overwhelmed in your day this will really help limit that.

The Greens is a super food supplement I personally take every morning to flood my body with all the good stuff. A scoop of Greens in a big glass of water and my body and mind is being nourished before I even leave the kitchen. We actually created our own Unbreakable Greens for our members so that they could get good tasting, top level nutrition for a reasonable price. That is how much I personally rate the benefit of drinking them first thing.

So that's the body covered. Now we move on to the mind. The mind uses a huge amount of energy and usually it is tired, overwhelmed and thinking stressed, reactive thoughts. If we are thinking stressed reactive thoughts, we take stressed reactive actions.

JOURNALING

In Unbreakable we are known for our journaling. In fact, all our members are sent our Unbreakable Journal when they join one of our programs. The Journal is laid out in such a way as to help prompt them to journal in the best way. In fact, I would go so far as to say that our journal is the key to becoming Unbreakable. It guides the user to check in daily with all of the strategies laid out in this book.

Think of journaling like a gym for the mind. A daily training that gets your brain reps in and allows you to train your brain to work better. You will literally train it to focus on better things, think better thoughts and create better feelings.

I will say this though. A lot of journaling does not help people because we do it wrong. Yep there you go I said it, people are journaling in a way that really doesn't help. I will tell you why.

If you have ever been told to write down how you feel you will know how frustrating that can be right? You wake up... Write down how stressed, anxious and afraid you are and what happens? You start to feel it even more. Why? Because of this law:

What you place your attention on grows.

So, if you wake up and place your attention on how stressed you feel then you will feel even more stressed. Consequently, there you are again; back in the centre of Struggle 1 and unable to see beyond where you are! You have to find ways to place your attention on the good things in your life, the things you love, the things you appreciate, the way you want to feel, what's going well for you. When you do that, you will start to grow that and that BUILDS mental energy rather than sucking it away from you.

MEDITATION AND BREATHING

A few Years ago, I sat in a small group of men waiting to learn about meditation when a lady monk walked in; Parashanti was her name. I was immediately taken by her. She had such an aura, she looked so peaceful and happy, and I felt so relaxed and at ease around her. That day in 4 hours she changed the course of my life. I was on a tough 3-day event called Unleashed where you took part in combat, intense physical training, huge mental challenges and a lot of soul searching. I didn't expect 4 hours with a monk to change my life, but it really did. She taught me the greatest gift I have ever been given;

You are not your thoughts. You just have them.

I walked away with the ability to be aware of thoughts, yet not get caught up in them. She gave me the power to understand that not everything you think is true. She gave a 28-year-old man a sense of freedom and peace of mind that I had so desperately longed for. I never saw her again, and not long after that event she died. A beautiful woman, who did beautiful work.

Meditation will allow you to set yourself free of thoughts and take you from the reactive servant of your mind, to the master and most importantly, the creator.

In Unbreakable our members aim to meditate or practice a form of breathing daily. Unbreakable members get constant guidance and support inside our own meditation program.

To help you, in this book I will explain a simple and powerful form of breathing for you to try. Just don't underestimate it or bomb it off as some kind of hippy stuff that doesn't work for you. It's a tried and tested practice that will transform your mind.

61

So now we move to the soul and your emotional energy.

All day long we give to the people we care about. All day long we notice how we feel and don't feel, and that emotional rollercoaster is exhausting. We can't give what we don't have. Investing in our emotional energy is not only enjoyable, it's a must if we want to give the people we love our best as well.

SOMETHING FOR YOU

Something for me? I hear you say. I can't possibly do something for me. I have so many people to look after, work that needs doing. Go on, you know you were thinking it. Of all the things we ask people to do in our Unbreakable Program this causes the most resistance. You would have thought I'd asked someone to eat a Crocodile's Testicle, (yes, I may have just been watching I'm A Celebrity....) It's resisted and resisted because we feel guilty for doing things for ourselves, and not only that but we also can't remember what it is we actually like doing anymore. We have been looking after everyone else for so long that our needs just weren't important. Yet they are important. Like I keep saying, you can't give what you don't have. Simply taking a little time each day to do something for you will do wonders for your happiness, your self-worth and your esteem. You will feel a rise in your energy levels, and you will start using your brain again.

So, what could you do each day for you? Maybe it's some kind of self-care? Reading? A hobby? ('What's that?' I hear you say!) Maybe you could learn something new.

Folks in our groups do anything from getting their nails done, reading, baths, walking, listening to music, playing music, ANYTHING that is just for you. Yes, you may have a tinge of guilt at the start, but you will also see that wear off and be replaced by a feeling of worth.

I like to play golf with the old man, which usually means I'll also be in for an earful. I never know what about.... But it is guaranteed. One thing I will say is this though. We do go through patches where we don't golf as much as I'd like, and I find myself using that age-old excuse: TIME. Yet, if I'm honest, the real reason is that I don't protect the time. I love Golf Fridays. Yet I let it slide. My brother says, 'If it's important you will find a way. If not, you will find an excuse' I like that. I think we also find excuses for the important stuff as well. We like to justify things, and so I set out to CREATE time for what is important to me. So, if you catch yourself making excuses for not doing what's important to you and hear the words, "I can't" start to come out of your mouth, maybe ask, "How can I?" You will be surprised how much we can make happen when we set our mind to it.

SOMETHING FOR SOMEONE ELSE

I can hear you again. You are saying, "but I do loads for other people," and I am sure you do. This is slightly different though compadre. You see I'm not talking about the running about for others. I'm talking doing something that you don't have to do but choose to do.

I'm talking an ACT of appreciation to someone with two simple rules: You don't need recognition or praise for it and, there is no personal agenda there.

Why do I say this? Well, I find that very often we really do give to receive. We want that 'thank you', that recognition back. I also find very often we like to moan about how much we do for folks, and how it's never appreciated but the fact of the matter is we do it because we like to feel wanted. Our ego loves the recognition, and at that point is it really giving to give? So, this is different. This is an act of appreciation to someone, without the need for something coming back.

What do people do? Send messages to loved ones each day telling them what they love about them with no need or reply. Leave notes around the house, put notes in kids lunch boxes. Call old friends out the blue. Leave bigger tips than normal somewhere. Send little videos to people. Do something for someone, knowing that they will never know that it was you.

Trust me on this. When you give with no need for something in return your emotional bank account will overflow with happiness and appreciation. So will your relationships, as you become the change you want to see.

Creating power is a vital step in making your vision for life a reality.

The old way of trying to struggle your way through action you don't really want to take but feel you have to is outdated and its broken. It flat out doesn't work.

You don't have to suffer your way to success. You don't have to feel awful to make things happen. You don't need someone else to motivate you for more will power.

You can go another way. You can CREATE power. You can make time for yourself and invest in your bank accounts. You can feel energetic, confident, loved and enthusiastic. When you come from that place, your actions will be inspired actions. The next action will simply be a stepping-stone to the next best thing. You will feel a little more ease in what you are doing. You will feel powerful and passionate.

Remember: Change requires you to be greater than your current reality.

To BE greater than your current reality you have to know what that looks like and have a VISION for your future.

To be greater than your current reality, you have to get out of Survival and feel greater than you do now. That takes Unbreakable Energy.

The following Energy rituals will help you FEEL greater.

Action step 2: The Morning Primer

A simple routine that takes 10-15 minutes and will leave you energised, motivated calm and confident.

Every Morning:

MOVEMENT: 100 reps of bodyweight exercises or any movement for 4-10 minutes.

It can be 25 squats - 25 sit ups. X 2. Any variation you like of anything.

HYDRATION: Drink a pint of water or Greens before you leave the house.

BREATHING: Set a timer for 5 minutes and practice what we call heart breathing

Close your eyes. Concentrate on the part of your chest that your heart is in and then just breathe naturally through there. Every 3-4 breaths simply think of the word love. It will shift you from stress and fear to love.

JOURNAL - Write down five things you appreciate about your life.

Simply thinking and noting what you have to appreciate will raise your mental and emotional energy massively.

Action Step 3: Evening Ritual 5/5/5

There are books everywhere which encourage us to focus on planning our mornings, which is great, but in doing this alone, I noticed a trend beginning to develop. Very often before I went to bed, I started planning the next day in my head, and very often I would predict feeling crap in the morning. I would worry and stress about what I had to do and would worry and stress with equal desperation about what I hadn't done.

Sure enough, when I woke up, I felt exactly as I predicted and picked up where I left off the night before. My morning routine would soon shift me back into alignment, but I couldn't help but wonder. What if I didn't wake up feeling that way? Along came the Evening Ritual.

BREATHING: Practice another 5 minutes of the heart breathing. The results for me were incredible. I slept better, woke feeling better and my morning primer became a top up and worked even more.

JOURNAL: Every night before bed write down the 5 best bits of your day that day and next to them the positive emotions they made you feel. Then 5 ways you want to feel the next day.

Tomorrow I want to feel _____ when I wake up tomorrow, I want to feel _____ after finishing work.

So why does this work so well?

Well, if we go to bed every night expecting to feel crap when we wake up, we are planting the seeds of expectation and our mind carries that intent into the next day.

So, you are now simply planting seeds you would like to see. You are now taking some control. When you add to that the great feelings you get from

Focusing on the best bits of your day you get a nice cocktail of thoughts and feelings that go to work in your sleep.

NOTE: These are basic habits. In our Unbreakable program we teach more advanced tools and rituals such as meditation and focus techniques, but for the sake of this book we wanted you to have things you could get on and do now that will make a difference.

Struggle 3

Negativity and Battling the Mind

Changing stuff in life is hard. I mean we can dress it up how we want, but no matter how skilled we are it's still difficult and there is good reason for that. Getting a new result will require taking new actions.

So, we have to do different. Of course, to do different you have to make a different choice, and that requires different thinking.

Changing our results will always come down to thinking different. That is where the problem comes, because by age 35, 95% of who we are is a set of automated unconscious habits and that includes the way you think. By habit I mean things we do unconsciously; things we do without thinking. The body knows better than us how to do it, so we no longer need to think about it. By who we are I mean how we think, feel and act.

Even more alarming is, it is said we have roughly 70,000 thoughts a day and you can't remember thinking all of those can you? If we are having 70,000 thoughts a day, most of which we are unaware of, and 95% of them are just an automated program, it's easy to see why change is so hard. If you imagine yourself as being like a computer- the program is running us, and we aren't even aware it's happening.

We keep thinking the way we always have, so we keep making the same decisions, taking the same actions, having the same experiences and then get the same results. Those things that you find quite easy in life, will have a useful program running smoothly and supporting that. Anything that you find really hard work; you have a program that doesn't support it. Simple as that.

Change requires new thinking or new 'programs.' It requires creating a new 95% that supports what you want.

The brain creates programs in two ways.

1 – Repetition

Think of the way you learn any habit. Let's use driving. When you were learning to drive you had to really concentrate. You were thinking intently about what you were doing. Every little detail you thought through. After a few years you are driving along chatting to your mate and just driving. You no longer think through every gear change and mirror check. Yet you are still doing it. Why? It's a habit. It's a program running away in the background.

It's the same with anything, including thinking. If you keep thinking thoughts like 'I'll never be fit', 'I'm useless', 'I'm not good enough', 'I can't change', the more you repeat those things; the more you repeat actions that back those theories of yours up. The more you listen to and repeat that negative internal chatter, the more you create a program around that negative mindset.

2 – Hypnosis.

I'm not talking about someone getting you up on stage and hypnotizing you to act like a chicken every time you hear the phone ring, however, it is the same principle. There is a well-known saying from the Greek philosopher Aristotle, "Give me a child until he is seven, and I will show you the man." (Of course, you CAN change who you are, that is what this whole book is about.) But what did he mean? Well up until roughly the age of 7, a human being will spend most of their time in Theta brainwave cycles. Those in a hypnotic or meditative state and animals' brainwaves are also mainly in this frequency. It could be said that the years between 0 – 7 are our programming years; where we are in a super-learning state and are open to suggestion. We are literally creating programs in our brain based on what we see and hear. Programs that root themselves deeply within us.

The reality is, if you grow up in a family where things are stressful, then you will struggle around those particular stressors as an adult.

So, what does this have to do with change? Here is what I really want you to place your attention on for a minute:

You CANNOT create consistent change fighting that program.

In fact, fighting it makes it even worse because the more attention you give something the worse it gets. Many of us say we want to get rid of our negative thoughts. Well, let me tell you this:

The only way to destroy something is to create something new and make that old thinking obsolete.

The crazy thing is, that the more we set out on making changes the louder the programs become. The louder the negative thoughts are. They dig in even harder, because nothing wants to die in life, and these programs are no different. You may well have experienced this. You are doing well making changes and then the voice seems to go up a gear. Many people think this is a sign it isn't working. I like to remind our Unbreakable members it's the opposite. That old way of thinking and being is dying, and it is clinging on for dear life. If we lack the skills to deal with it, then you know what happens; we give in to the temptation. For a moment we satisfy the cravings, soon followed by the familiar feelings of guilt, shame, self-loathing until normal order is resumed. The old program is back in charge.

At this point it is crucial to have a level of training and to be creating a new program.

That negative chatter is a sign that you are moving in the right direction. If you can learn the skills required to ignore it, you will not only become stronger, but you will commit to your future and that voice will quieten until it is replaced by one of belief, confidence and desire.

Your success in crossing the void, in moving beyond the negative chatter, relies on not giving in to that voice.

Just before moving on to the Unbreakable Focus section, I want to say a little something about other people's negativity.

So, you are mastering your internal negative chatter... But what about other people? I get this question a lot. People telling me that they are starting to do great, but that those around them are negative and bring them down.

What about other people's opinions? What do you do with 'negative' comments? Here we go. Negative comments in a nutshell.

(Bear in mind, I get a ton!)

1 - A negative comment is quite simply someone's opinion it's not FACT.
2 - Their opinion is made up of how they think and feel about a subject as far as THEIR life goes.
3 - They are now expressing how they feel about their life and what they would do.
4 - So it's all about THEM.
5 - You have no control over this.
6 - How they feel has nothing to do with you.
7 - Now you know that they are simply expressing how they feel, ask yourself: how do you have to feel about your life to put somebody else down?
7 - Put yourself in their shoes.
8 - This doesn't make it OK or right, or you wrong.
9 - But hey; now you have some empathy.
10 - Empathy will stop you making it all about you.
11 - At this point it's nice to remember that anyone can have an opinion, but you don't have to listen and let that dictate what you do or how you feel.
12 - Carry on with your day.
13 - One last thing, Colombo. Sometimes people have a point.

Remember not all negative comments are criticism, sometimes they are just feedback that we can use to get better.

Opinions. We all have them. I just gave you mine.

When it comes to those folks who put you down, knock you and always seem to make comments, remember: It says more about where they are at, than where you are.

Smile.
Empathise.
Move on.

At this juncture, I would also make the point that it is just as important for you not to get into a state trying to convince everyone else that what you are doing is right and that they are wrong. You don't need to prove anyone else wrong to know that what you are doing is the right thing for you.

I had a great little insight into this very thing one night when I was out.

Like, out on a night out... out. I was also sober. Man, you see some cool stuff when you are sober and everyone else is drunk. For one, people don't stop taking photos. I don't mean the odd group photo either, I mean every 5 seconds there is a photo being taken. I'm sure that photo looks great after 16 filters have been added, but man, it looks weird from the outside. Some kind of leaning, screwing up your face, weird shit going on.

t also probably looks like these folks are having a great time if you are sat at home on your tod. Don't worry, in between their photos they are generally sat there on their phones ignoring each other. I just read that back and I sound pretty dam old, (although I already came to the conclusion I was old when I thought we were in a club, but it was actually just a bar.). I started thinking things like 'This music is too loud. I can't have a conversation with anyone.'

So, what is the point in telling you all this? I'm an each to their own kinda guy... Sure, we all notice and think, that looks like it sucks, but If you aren't hurting anyone and it makes you happy then crack on. I also gave up trying to convince people of my points of view ages ago.

The world is full of contrasting opinions and ideas.

That's cool. What I think is a good time, may be completely different to someone else. Who is right? Who is wrong? The reality is. Who cares? Everyone is doing what they think is right for them.

We don't need to all agree to get on, and we don't need others to agree with us for what we are doing to be right for us. So much energy is wasted on all that nonsense. So many issues arise from trying to please everyone else and get them to agree to back up our way. Moral of the tale. Be true to you. Find what works for you and allow others to do the same. You may well experience a massive sense of freedom.

Fighting your mind. Arguing with others. Distracting your mind. Even trying to out sweat it with tons of exercise is not the answer to creating a healthy mindset. Training it is. To do that we use the two ways we made the old, existing programs. repetition and hypnosis. The next section of this book is dedicated to repetition, using the Unbreakable Focus method, but first a little story. (No golf or Dad in this one, sorry.)

The Valley of Doom

There comes a point in any effort to get across the void to your goal where you reach what in Unbreakable, we call the Valley of Doom.

It's the point of the journey when things are getting tougher, your results are slowing, enthusiasm is dropping, and you feel like quitting. You can't see a way out, and your behaviors and thoughts start drifting back to your lowest standards. You start to long to go back to where you used to be with stories like, 'it wasn't so bad before...'

We want to quit.

I have reached that point many a time. Most memorably in a race called the Fan Dance. The Fan Dance is an SAS route march across the Brecon Beacons at night with 18kg of weight in your bag. It's tough. It's not particularly far but the added weight and three huge climbs make it a tough task.

We set off at about 10pm up Pen Y Fan and down the other side. You then have a fair bit of flat ground before you attack another steep hill.

At this point you turn back on yourself, down the hill and across the flat before reaching what is known as Jacob's Ladder.

It got to about 2am, my legs were killing, my joints and knees had taken a battering from the weight and my body wanted to sleep.

I hit the valley. I wanted to quit. It was dark and no matter how many steps I took, I didn't seem to be seeing the light at the top of the peak.

My mind was telling me, "It's stupid. My knees hurt too much. It's too hard."

I was all on my own at this point, the mate I started with was down the bottom and I was fed up.

I stop. At this point I've made my mind up, I have quit. We all reach this point. The point of no return. The point where we get to decide. We get to choose if we want to see the change or give up.

No matter what goal you have you will experience the valley.

It's inevitable. It's part of the process. I'm not saying you have to suffer your way to success, what I am saying is you will reach a point where you don't feel like you can go on.

But you must. This is your chance. The valley is where you get to put everything we have spoken about in to practice.

It's where the vision you created comes in to its own as you start to cling to that instead of retreat back to square one. It's where we need our Power Rituals more than ever to keep us moving and it's the perfect time to use your Focus Skills and turn that negative self-talk in to an Unbreakable Mindset.

This same valley hit me when after 12 months of renovating a house with nothing to show for it but bare walls, one finished room and the back of the building missing. On top of that, there was no money left.

Everything in your mind wants to give in…

But it forged me as a person, and I know it will forge you too.

That night at the bottom of Jacob's Ladder I shifted my attention to why I was doing it. I shifted it to how far I had come. I altered my perspective from "there is no point, this is too hard" to "I can do this. I want to do this." I powered on up the hill one stride at a time into the morning with renewed strength.

You will face many valleys of doom. It's not a sign that you are failing. It's a chance to learn lessons, it's a chance to build resolve, it's a chance to get better and bring out the person you know you are deep down.

Of course, you can choose to suffer through it. Or avoid it all together. But an Unbreakable uses it to their advantage and comes out of it stronger.

SOLUTION 3

Unbreakable Focus

If negative programs are what are holding you back, then creating Unbreakable Focus is what will propel you forward into the void of change and they require Unbreakable Focus to create.

Think back to when you were born. I mean, I know you can't remember it, but you were still there my friend. No one is born with a lack of confidence, likewise no one is born anxious or afraid of failure. We learn these things as we grow up. Without getting into a whole 'nature/nurture' debate, it's safe to say that they are mostly all learnt and acquired behaviors. So, if we can learn to feel afraid of other's opinions, if we can learn to resist change and feel anxious, then we can unlearn it too. In fact, you can train yourself to feel confident and focused.

As we discussed in the last chapter, one of the main ways we learn is repetition. So now it's time to get it on your side by training a new program everyday using the following system.

The Unbreakable Focus Principles:

Appreciation
Awareness
Attention.

They are the three A's of Unbreakable Focus that you will want to understand and master so that you can train a new program and negative chatter becomes a thing of the past.

APPRECIATION

Most negative chatter is based in fear and stress. Any time you notice yourself feeling something you don't want, look at the reason behind it. It's always fear. Anxiety comes from fear. Overwhelm from fear. Anger and frustration from fear. You get the picture. At the root, all these are fear-based emotions. Now, notice the thoughts that you consider negative, they too will be based out of those emotions. One of the best things you can do to get out of the negative chatter mindset is to start to cultivate a state of appreciation. Appreciation for who you are, appreciation for what you do have in life, appreciation for how far you have come. What you appreciate, appreciates. Constantly being in lack will only ever create more lack in your life. Learning to appreciate the small things we do have will always lead to more.

AWARENESS

Awareness is an incredible skill to learn. We live in a pretty self-aware world these days. Lots of people aware of their problems, their flaws and what's not going well. Not so many of us are aware of what we are doing well, our great qualities and the opportunities that are available to us. You will want to train yourself to be aware of the useful things in your life. Learning to focus on the possibilities for yourself. Learning to focus on the opportunities you have. You really will notice you get what you expect in life. Expect your week to be hard, it will usually be hard. Expect people to be annoying; they will be. Foresee big obstacles in life and you will find them. You get what you look for in life. A big part of using that to your benefit is learning to open up your awareness.

ATTENTION

What you place your attention on grows. That is a fact. The more you look at something, the bigger it gets. So, learning to place your attention on the useful is a skill that will propel you forward. You will know that if you ever find yourself in a position where you have heart your heart set on something in life. Let's use a car, for example. Very often you will decide you like a certain car. Maybe you start looking at it online or whatever, and all of a sudden you notice it on the roads. The more you see them and give them your attention the more and more you see. This is the power of your attention. They have always been there but now your mind is actively looking for them you see more and more of them.

The three A's are always being used. The more we learn to actively use them to train our thoughts, the better-quality programs we create.

Usually, though, these thoughts are just left to their own devices. Let's look at how these A's normally work out for us.

Just think of any normal day in our lives. As soon as we wake up, we start to feel about for the familiar feelings we always have, waiting for them to pop up; "oh yep it's there, there is my usual exhaustion, there is my normal anxiety about the day ahead." We come to our senses and most of us reach for our phone, we scroll through the usual suspects, email, Facebook, WhatsApp, already giving our ATTENTION to everything other than useful things before we are even half awake. Then we wonder off to the shower already thinking about what needs doing today what we didn't get done yesterday, putting ourselves in LACK. We shower the exact same way, try and get everyone else sorted and packed off to where they need to be, having the same conversations or arguments as we usually do. Already we are feeling a state of lack and stress, placing our attention on things that we can't control or that don't serve us. We woke up, jumped on the treadmill of life and the programs continued to run our day for us. From here on its Groundhog Day and we just keep reaffirming that old program that keeps running us.

We are in lack not Appreciation
We are not aware of anything beyond what's happening.
We are putting our Attention on things that don't help us.

Examples of negativity are everywhere. You see them every day; big and small. So, here is a story to illustrate my point……. Excuse me while I take a minute to tell you another story about the main man himself: my Dad.

One Golf Friday, my Old Man and I hit the fairways and for a change he was beating me as we were heading into the last hole. I've got to be honest; he was playing pretty damn well. Whatever I did and however good a hole I had, he pulled it out the bag. Heading into the last hole I wasn't expecting much, but while walking to the tee he started a rant; "I bloody hate this tee... I always play it awful; I reckon it's the line of the trees, it sends my drive left every time!" He tees up and BOSH! The ball goes flying over the trees into someone's garden. "I bloody knew it!" He proceeded to hand me the game with an awful last hole. The lesson is simple. You get what you expect a lot of the time and the way you talk to yourself is crucial. Your actions will always back up yourself image. Read that again. It is why it's so important to think of yourself in a way that helps. Think you are a failure? Your actions will eventually back up your theory. Think you are a bad person? Your actions will catch up and one place I used to do this more than any was before I went off to sleep. I'd always start predicting I would wake up feeling crap. Or I would start to worry about everything I had to do and how I wouldn't get it done.

Guess what? I was always right.

So, I started doing the following:

1 - I'd write down the best little bits of my day in a notepad and I would always include noting down the improvements in how I felt that day.

2 – I'd write down a mini little ideal day tomorrow.

How I would feel when I woke up.
How I would feel doing the things I wanted.
How I would feel at the end of the day.

Kind of like a little story. Not a checklist of jobs.   Over time my days started getting better. I was changing what I expected to happen. If you struggle in the mornings this my friend is GOLD.

The answer to training a new program is using the A's to your advantage and consciously training them. Enter the Focus tools.

We have tons of tools in our Unbreakable programs to train your focus. Ones for really building your attention around positive things and raising your energy in good ways. Some that will change your thoughts around to more useful ones, creating visions and overcoming obstacles. On a day to day basis, our Unbreakable Journal really helps here, however, something that you can use right now is the Focus Wheel.

Action Step 4: The Focus Wheel

Step 1 – Take 10 slow deep breaths as you learnt in the Heart Breathing. This will create some space and get you off the treadmill of life for a few minutes.

Step 2 – Write something you want in the middle of the wheel. Or simply start by writing 'today.' (Wheel example on next page)

Step 3 – Continue this breathing and fill out the wheel by writing something you appreciate about that subject or that you would like to happen be true about that subject. This will start training your attention and awareness on the useful things in life.

Step 4 – Go back through and read it all while continuing to breathe.

Step 5 – Smile you just trained your mind.

In this way, you place your attention in on what you can do not what you can't do. What is good and not what is negative. All of a sudden you are back in power.

That is a trainable skill. That is Unbreakable focus.

Building a state of appreciation. Looking for possibilities not problems. Placing your attention on what you can do not what you can't, upon what you appreciate and not what you don't.

This tool will allow you to move away from the negative chatter holding you back. Like we said in the previous chapter, you will never outperform how you think and feel. So, we have to shift our focus around that when the negative chatter starts to halt our progress.

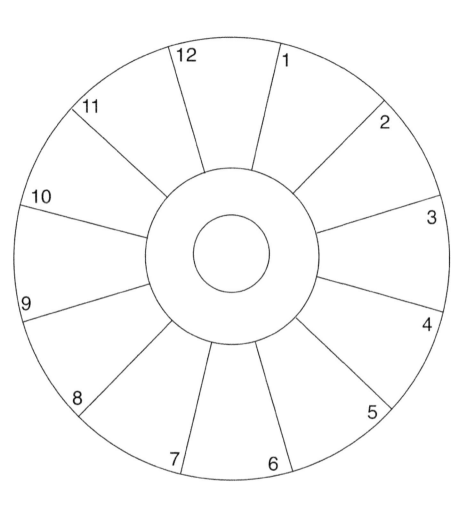

CHAPTER 4

Overcoming Obstacles and Setbacks

One way of looking at life is that everything happens to us and that dictates how we feel and what we get out of life. Our external reality shapes who we are. That, my friends, is a very reactive, almost victim-based model; a passive model. However, another model, the Unbreakable model is:

Who we are shapes our reality.

That is a liberating creative model that puts you in control. How we choose to think, feel and act shapes the experiences we have. Sure, things happen beyond our control and we don't create that. We do, however, choose the meaning of what happens. We get to choose the meaning of everything in life, because life is meaningless until we choose the meaning ourselves. That's how two people can go through an identical situation and both take completely different things from it. For example, if more than one person reads this book, (let's hope so, eh) you will both be reading the exact same words, but you could have completely different experiences and take completely different things from it. One of you could love it. One could hate it. What decides the difference is how you choose to think and feel about it. The meaning you give these words.

Why am I sharing this? Because a crucial part in creating an Unbreakable Focus is learning emotional intelligence. For me, this is the ability to overcome these obstacles and setbacks and continue on your path towards your Vision. For me this is a skill everyone should practice and learn and something we teach a great deal in the Unbreakable 30-day Challenges we run. You will always hit road bumps on your way towards what you want. Learning to roll with these bumps, not let them send you in to a tailspin and set you back for days is a crucial step in not only creating change, but also in creating a healthy mindset. Let's look at how this plays out for most of us.

Something happens. Say we don't get the result we want. Someone says something that we take personally, we get criticised. Let's use the example of going for a new job.

I go for the job and I find out I haven't got it. Straight away I start to give this meaning. This meaning is a choice, but very often it doesn't seem that way. Say I decide it means I am not good enough, and I start thinking, "that's it, I'll never get a job I want. Everyone will think I am stupid now." We create this meaning and a nice image that we are a failure. From that point the brain sends out a load of little chemical messengers into the body called emotions and I FEEL a failure. If I continue to keep thinking about it, I'll keep feeling that way, and I will start to find more areas in my life in which I believe that I am a failure. I may start to avoid situations where I could fail. Now my emotions are defining me. Many of us then allow these feelings to govern the rest of our life, forever defining ourselves a failure. That all started through choosing to give a certain meaning to an event. This is why emotional intelligence is such a powerful skill to learn.

Using the same scenario, imagine if I got the news that I didn't get the job and decided on a different meaning. Maybe I choose thoughts like, "What a great experience that was, at least I have some feedback to improve on. I'll go into the next interview even better prepared."

All of a sudden, I am creating a better meaning. I am getting much different feelings and I will end up taking much better actions. All this through choosing a more useful meaning.

Victor Frankl talks heavily about this in his book, 'Man's Search for Meaning.' In brief, he was in a Nazi war camp and survived. He went on to write about it and two quotes in his book stood out for me.

Between stimulus and response there is a space. In that space is our power to choose our response. In our response lies our growth and our freedom.

And.

When we are no longer able to change a situation, we are challenged to change ourselves

Although I used the small example of not getting a job and choosing the meaning, very often it's a big thing in someone's life that sends them on a downward tailspin.

Often, we are justified in how we feel, yet there will come a time when we have to ask ourselves the tough question; "Do I want to continue to view this in a way that keeps holding me back from the future I want?" If the answer is no, then it's the meaning that we need to start to change. This doesn't mean we have to make it positive. It simply means we have to choose a meaning that moves us forward not one that keeps us stuck. To move forward, we need to CHOOSE a meaning that is useful to us.

As with all things in Unbreakable, we like to practice this skill every time we hit an obstacle or setback or an event that throws us off by using a simple tool.

Action Step 5: The Reframe Tool

Step 1 – Take 10 deep Heart Breaths to create some space.

Step 2 – Grab a pen and paper and answer the following questions:

1 - What's happened?

2 - What meaning are you giving it?

3 - How's that making you feel right now?

4 - What is a more useful meaning you could give it that would move you forward?

5 - How does that meaning make you feel?

6 - What would you like out of this situation now?

7 - What's a small step you can take to get closer to this?

Step 3 – Take the action

CHAPTER 5

Being Unbreakable

In the words of Frank Sinatra, 'and now the end is near and so I face the final curtain' ...I do love me some Frank. In true Unbreakable fashion for the end we go back to the start and the title of this book. What is being Unbreakable and how do you go about 'Becoming Unbreakable'?

Being Unbreakable is when you take the role of active creator in your life. No longer a participant in a game that you don't want to play. It's about being the best you. The you that you know you want to be.

I truly believe anyone can BE who they want to be, and that when you do, you will create a life you want to BE in as well. You don't need to be special, gifted or lucky. You simply need to follow a system. A system that we are proving works time and time again.

At the start of the book I laid out some stats that we have taken over the last few years. None of the people involved had anything going on different to you. They are from all walks of life. Some arrived struggling, maybe having gone through life altering experiences before joining us. Some of our number were super successful and flying high but wanting more. Yet they were ALL able to completely upgrade their life because they had a system to follow. A simple, (not always easy) system and a united cause: To create change and get more out of their life.

I know you can join them in creating the changes you want in your own life if you follow the system too.

I know that if you want to change your life then you will want to stop running from what it is you don't want and start running towards a VISION of your future and what you do want.

I know that survival mode is killing your ability to create change and that through simply mastering your ENERGY and making small deposits in your energy accounts you can go on to ease out of survival and start creating changes.

Last but not least I know that battling your mind is fighting a lost cause. That the only way to destroy an old way of thinking is by creating a new one. That will only happen when you create FOCUS and work with it not against it.

That is the Unbreakable system.

Vision + (Energy x Focus) = Unbreakable

It's the ability to be GREATER than your current reality.
It's the path to becoming WHO you want and in doing so create a life you want.
A path that has laid out for you.
All that is left is for you to take the next best step.

Unbreakable: When you know exactly who you are and what you are worth, completely in control of how you think and feel, saying fuck you to normal and making the impossible a reality.

Action Step 6: Do the Work

So, what can you do next with all this info and these action points?

1 - Go create your VISION by creating the perfect day.

2 - Start upping your ENERGY by hitting your routines.

3 - Keep FOCUSSED with the focus tool.

If you are the action taking type and want to be coached and mentored personally by me through the full Unbreakable Program, then email us on:

Unbreakablehq@gmail.com

Here you can get all the details about my famous 30-day Program, and you can send any questions or let us know how you are getting on.

So, now all that is left is for you to get yourself moving!

Time to get going my friend.

Printed in Great Britain
by Amazon